TWELVE 12 WAYS

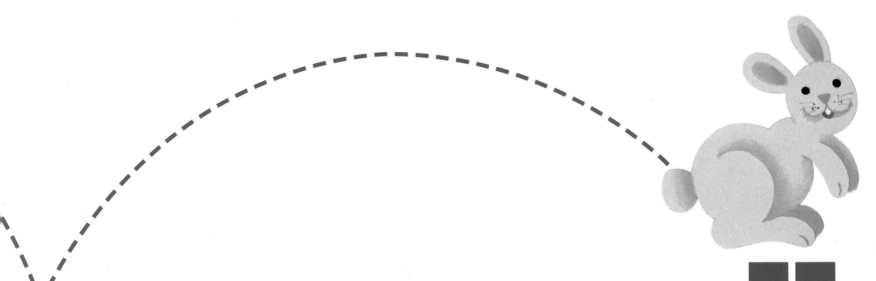

TO GET TO ELEVEN 11

Aladdin Paperbacks

12
WAYS
TO GET TO
11
—

Written
by
**EVE
MERRIAM**
•
Illustrated
by
**BERNIE
KARLIN**

1234567

The publisher deeply regrets the deaths of Eve Merriam and
Bernie Karlin as this book was being prepared for publication.

First Aladdin Paperbacks edition August 1996
Text copyright © 1993 by Eve Merriam
Illustrations copyright © 1993 by Bernie Karlin
Aladdin Paperbacks
An imprint of Simon & Schuster
Children's Publishing Division
1230 Avenue of the Americas
New York, NY 10020
Also available in a Simon & Schuster Books for Young Readers edition
Designed by Bernie Karlin
The text of this book was set in Avant Garde and Futura.
The illustrations were done in cut paper and colored pencil.
Manufactured in China
20 19 18 17 16 15
The Library of Congress has cataloged the hardcover edition as follows:
Merriam, Eve. Twelve ways to get to eleven
by Eve Merriam: illustrated by Bernie Karlin.
Summary: Uses ordinary experiences to present twelve combinations of numbers
that add up to eleven. Example: at the circus, six peanut shells and five pieces
of popcorn.   1. Addition—Juvenile literature.   2. Counting—Juvenile literature.
(1. Eleven (The number)   2. Addition.   3. Counting.)
1. Karlin, Bernie, ill.   II. Title.   III. Title: 12 ways to get to 11.
QA115.M47   1992   513.2   11—dc20
ISBN: 0-671-75544-7   91-25810
ISBN: 0-689-80892-5 (Aladdin pbk.)

8 9 10

12

For Del,
Karen and
Toby
—EM

In memory
of
Dr. L. John Adkins,
the greatest
teacher
I've
ever known;
and to
Ted Miñon
for
helping me.
—BK

11

ONE, TWO, THREE, FOUR, FIVE, SIX, SEVEN, EIGHT, NINE, TEN,

▪▪▪▪▪▪▪▪▪▪▪▪▪▪▪▪▪▪

TWELVE.

WHERE'S

ELEVEN?

Pick up
nine pinecones
from the forest floor
and two acorns.

At the
circus,
six
peanut
shells

and
five
pieces
of
popcorn.

Out of the magician's hat:
four banners,
five rabbits,
a pitcher of water,
and a
bouquet of flowers.

Go past four corners and two traffic lights,

then past the house with two chimneys

and the garage with two cars
and a bicycle.

Now look, you're at Eleventh Street.

Six bites,

a core,

a stem,

and
three
apple
seeds.

On the boat are two masts,
a big and a little sail,
four life preservers,
a flag, a ladder and
an anchor.

Three turtles sleeping,
two frogs swimming,
one lily pad,
and five dragonflies
darting on top of the pond.

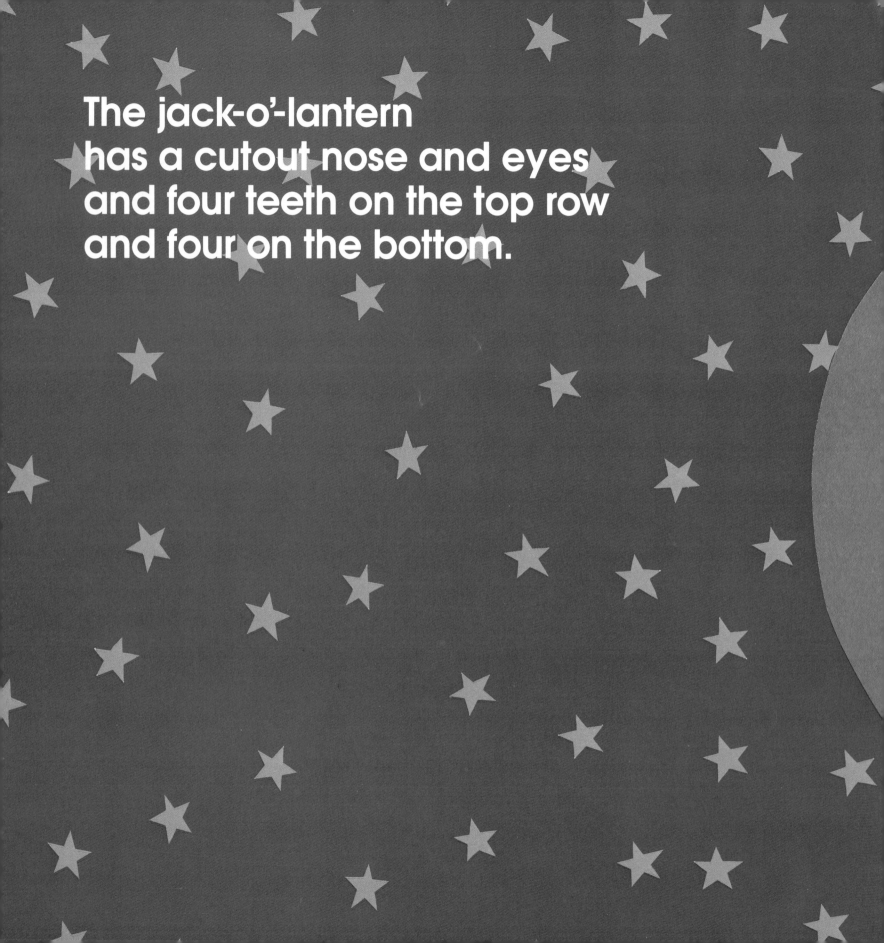

The jack-o'-lantern
has a cutout nose and eyes
and four teeth on the top row
and four on the bottom.

In the
mailbox:
seven letters,
two packages,
a mail-order
catalog,
and a
picture
postcard.

Three sets of triplets in baby carriages and a pair of twins in the stroller.

A sow
and ten
baby piglets.

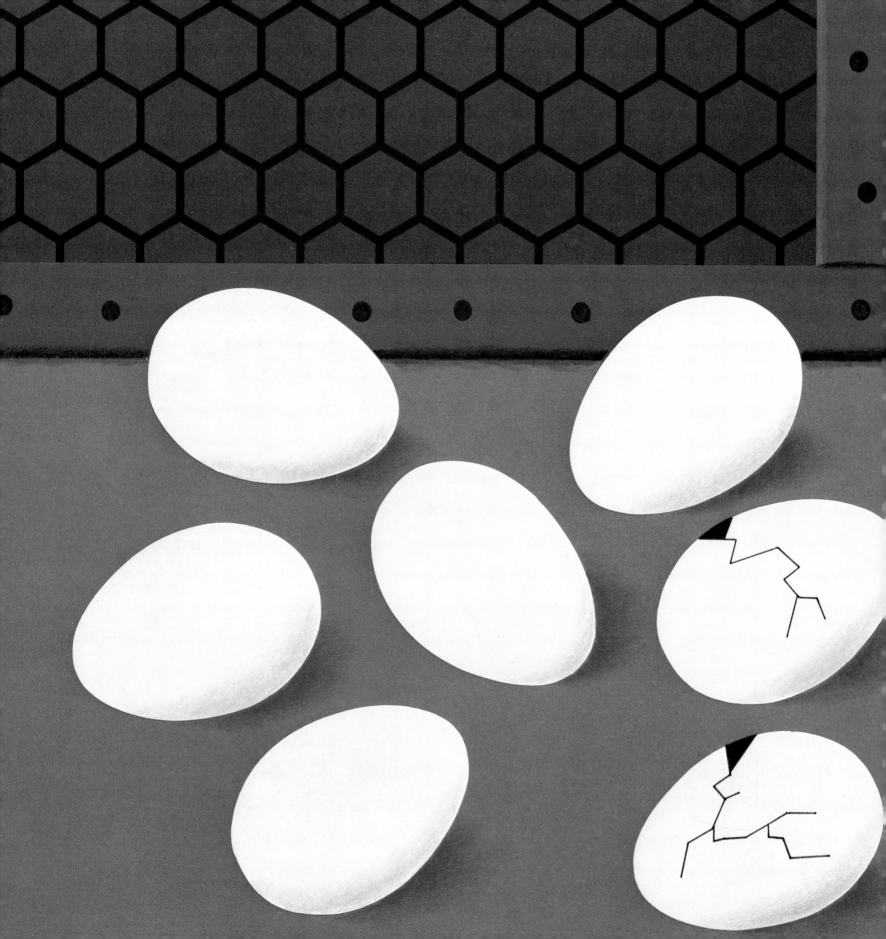

In the hen yard:
five eggs,
three cracking open,
two beaks poking out,
and one just hatched.